So... what IS an
Alpaca?

By
Joanne Louise Dell

So... what IS an Alpaca?

Copyright © 2016 Joanne Louise Dell. All rights reserved.
First paperback edition printed 2016 in the United Kingdom
A catalogue record for this book is available from the British Library.

ISBN 978-0-9935048-1-5

No part of this book shall be reproduced or transmitted in any form or by any means, electronic or mechanical, including photocopying, recording, or by any information retrieval system without written permission of the publisher.

Published by Abbotts View Publishing
For more copies of this book, please email:
Jo.dell@abbottsviewalpacas.co.uk
Tel: 07989 063595

Printed in Great Britain

Although every precaution has been taken in the preparation of this book, the publisher and author assume no responsibility for errors or omissions. Neither is any liability assumed for damages resulting from the use of this information contained herein.

So...what IS an Alpaca?

Caramel

An **Alpaca** is part of the **Camelid** family which includes **Llamas, Guanacos** and **Vicuña**. Alpacas and llamas were **domesticated** about 6000 years ago. Alpacas are **small, gentle** and **inquisitive** animals.

Where do Alpacas come from?

Alpacas come from **South America** where they live in the Altiplano (spanish for high plain) in **Peru, Chile** and **Bolivia**. There are about **3.5 million** alpacas in the world. About 3 million live in South America. Alpacas first arrived in the UK in the 1990's.

Map of the World, showing where alpacas originate from (Peru, Chile & Bolivia)

Are there different **breeds** of alpaca?

Suri alpaca (centre) Huacayas either side

There are two different **breeds** of alpaca: **Suri** (Soo-ri) and **Huacaya** (Wa-ky-ya). There are more Huacayas (c.95%) than Suris (c.5%) in the world. Huacayas have a thick crimpy teddy bear like fleece and need to be shorn every year. Suris fleece is flatter, finer and longer and Suris are usually shorn every two years.

How big is an alpaca?

Jo with Caramel, Cleo, Coco, Darcy, Delilah & Dot

An alpaca measures about **1 metre tall** at the withers (shoulders). An adult female **(Hembra)** weighs about **65kg**. An adult male weighs about **75kg**. A breeding male is called a **Macho** and a non breeding male a **Wether**

Are alpacas like sheep?

An alpaca is **bigger** than a sheep. Both grow a fleece and are **sheared** in Spring/early Summer. An alpaca fleece doesn't contain **lanolin** so isn't greasy. Alpaca fibres are **hollow** (good for trapping heat) and have **fewer scales** than sheep fibres, so less itchy.

Alpacas watching Greyface Dartmoor and Manx Loaghtan Sheep

What are alpacas bred for?

Alpacas are bred mainly for their fleece which is soft and luxurious, naturally fire resistant and hypoallergenic. There are 22 recognised colours. It can be spun into yarn for knitted items and woven and used in suits/clothing. Coarser fleece can be used in pillows or duvets or used for craft activities, for example felting.

Caramel's fleece

Kilimanjaro going for a walk

Their secondary use is **meat; low** in **cholesterol** and **fat** and **high** in **protein.** It is a red meat and has been likened to venison. In addition to fibre and meat, some alpaca farms welcome visitors and provide the opportunity to **walk an alpaca** on a **halter** and **lead.** **Halter fit** is **very important** as they have **short nasal bones** but are **nasal breathers.** An incorrect fit can compromise their breathing.

How do you **shear** an alpaca?

Alpacas are laid on their **side** to be sheared, rather than sitting on their rump, like sheep. Each of their legs is **tethered**.

The **blanket** (the premium fleece from neck to the tail) is removed first and bagged, and the fleece from the neck, belly and legs are usually bagged separately.

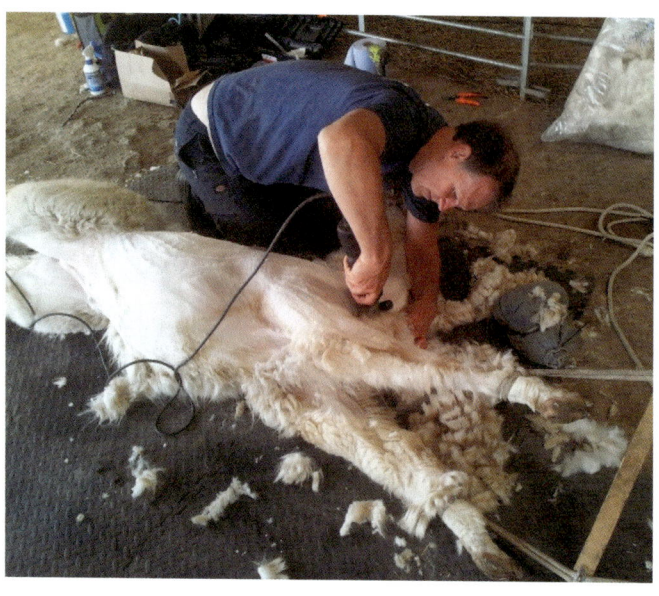

Alpaca being shorn

What do you do with the fleece?

Hand spinners love alpaca fleece and will spin it unwashed, because it is grease free. Large quantities have to be skirted (bits of hay and any guard hair removed) and then can be sent to a mill to be processed into yarn. Most alpaca mills use the worsted or semi-worsted process of spinning. Yarn spun from premium alpaca fleece is supremely soft, likened to cashmere and is luxuriously warm thanks to its long hollow fibres.

How long do alpacas **live** for?

An alpaca can live for about **15-20 years.**

They are **very sociable** animals and need friends.

A group of alpacas is called a **herd.**

Caramel at 1 year

Do alpacas get ill?

Delilah rolling in Diatomaceous earth

Like all animals, alpacas **do sometimes** get ill. But they are very good at hiding it! They need **vaccinations** every year and regular **worming.** They can be susceptible to mites, but love nothing more than a roll in some **diatomaceous earth** which helps keep mites at bay.

What do alpacas eat?

Alpacas are semi-ruminants but with 3 stomach compartments instead of 4. They survive mainly on grass and hay. Most owners also supplement them with a low protein mix which includes minerals and nutrients. Alpacas can be trained to eat from a hand or tray.

Kattia enjoying some alpaca food

How much land do you need to keep alpacas?

The recommendation is 3-5 alpacas per acre. But they are gentle on the pasture because of their soft padded feet. They choose communal dung piles, making them easier to clean up after and causing less contamination where they are grazing. Alpaca dung is an excellent fertiliser.

What's a **baby** alpaca called?

Cleo with mum, Kattia

A baby alpaca is called a **cria** and weighs between **6-8kg** at **birth**. Alpacas are **induced ovulators** so can be bred at any time, and breeders plan births for the warmer Spring/Summer months.

How long is an alpaca pregnant?

Pregnancy lasts about 11.5 months and twins are rare. Alpacas usually give birth during the early daylight hours.

Newborn cria, just moments old

Are alpacas friendly?

Nosy Lulu

Alpacas are really nosy! They just love to see what's going on and they often run over to meet visitors. They have very good eyesight so are great at spotting predators. They can be very effective flock guards for sheep/poultry keeping foxes at bay.

Can I **stroke** an alpaca?

Alpacas love to meet new people, but despite how **cuddly** and **fluffy** they look they **don't really like being stroked**. If taught from a young age to accept touch they will **tolerate** it but they don't really enjoy it! But because they are so nosy, they will come right over to check you out making them delightful animals to keep.

Orphaned Dolly enjoying a bottle of goats milk

Do alpacas have hooves?

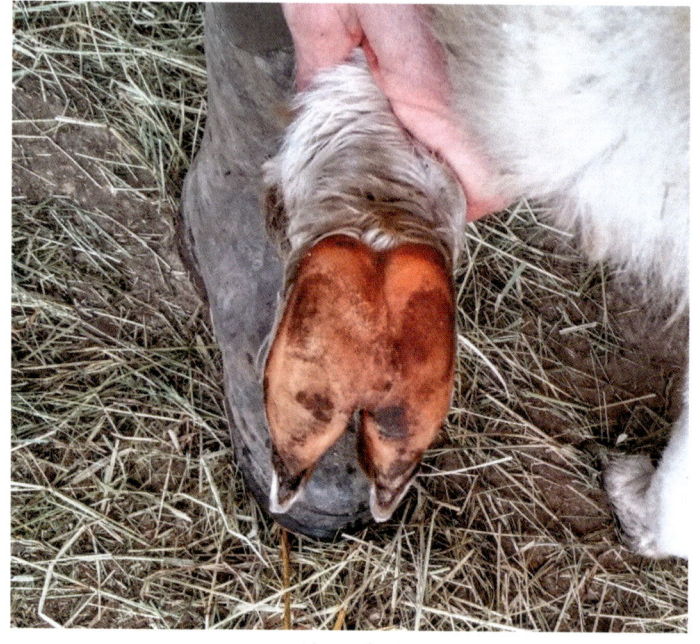

Alpaca foot

Alpacas don't have hooves but have **soft pads** with **two toenails** that need trimming about 4 times a year. The toenails of white/light alpacas seem to grow quicker than coloured alpacas. They don't generally suffer from foot rot, like other animals do.

Do alpacas **kick**?

Yes sometimes. They will **kick** back if they feel anything directly behind them. But because they only have soft feet it doesn't usually do too much damage, but can hurt!
Beware of the kick zone!

Casper, Charlie and Caramel

Do alpacas spit?

Lucinda, Dolly, Bambi, Delilah

Alpacas can spit but usually only when they are cross or scared. More often they "puff" a blow of air. They mainly puff at each other when they don't want to share their food or as a warning. They rarely puff or spit at humans, unless you get caught in the crossfire!

Do alpacas roar?

No! But they do make a variety of noises. They hum, when they are worried, they make an unusual alarm call if they see something they consider to be a predator and the males orgle when they mate, which is a most peculiar sound!

Do alpacas bite?

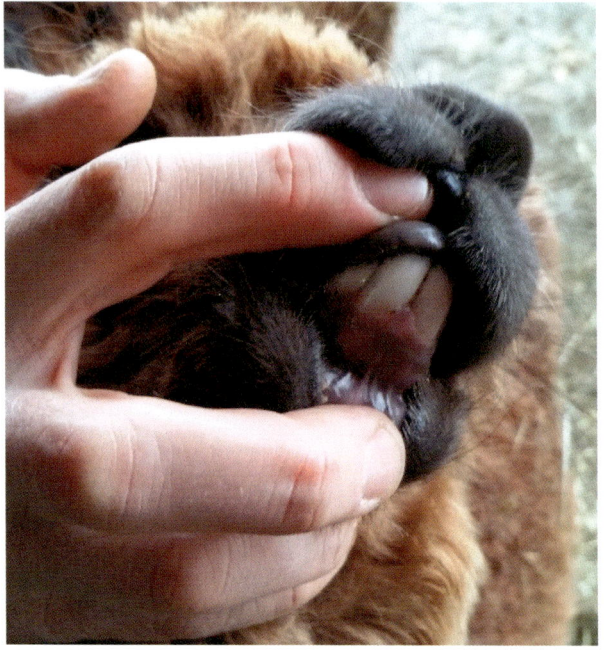

Dot showing her lower teeth and upper hard pad

No, alpacas don't usually bite but will sometimes nibble on your clothes to attract attention! They only have lower teeth at the front of their mouths with a hard upper pad. The males have fighting teeth further back, but these are trimmed at shearing so they can't do any damage.

Do you **milk** them?

No, unless we are trying to help a cria feed. Their milk is produced in **small** quantities; they don't "bag up" like other animals do. They have **4 teats** and when a cria feeds it feeds a little from each one. Cria are **weaned** at around 5/6 months.

Coco as a cria feeding mum Lucinda

Can alpacas live out all year?

Cleo cooling off

Yes! Alpaca fleece is an excellent insulator keeping them **warm** in the winter and **cool** in the summer. However they can **overheat** if they are not shorn before very hot weather so appreciate **shade** or **water** to cool off in. In the winter they need **protection** from rain and wind but don't mind cold at all.

Can you **ride** an alpaca?

No! The bone structure of an alpaca is really not strong enough. Llamas have been used as pack animals for 1,000's of years but they can only really carry about ¼ of their **weight**, making them ideal to **carry bags** but not people.

Llamas pictured in front of the Machu Picchu UNESCO World Heritage Site

Can you **train** alpacas?

Jo training a soggy Sweep

Most definitely! Alpacas respond well to **calm** and **gentle** handling. It is easier to train a young alpaca than an older one but it's important not to **overhandle** young cria. A **catch pen** made out of hurdles is an excellent way to work with them. Feed them in there, then close them in. If you chase them you will be outrun every time!

So... if you want to keep alpacas you will need:

- Land – with suitable fencing (4ft high)
- Water troughs or buckets
- Feeding troughs that can be lifted off the ground (to keep badgers out)
- Hay trough/rack
- Alpaca concentrated feed
- Halters and lead ropes
- Alpaca hurdles (4ft high)
- Foot rot shears for toenail clipping
- A shelter (if possible)
- A vet (preferably one familiar with camelids)
- An alpaca shearer's details (book early)
- Some common sense/sense of humour
- Time – you'll spend hours just watching/sitting with them!

Printed in Great Britain
by Amazon